Peacefully Loud
Sun Painted Waves

Kendall Thompson

Sunrisers

Sunrisers

For the sunriser, that enjoys distance running on the beach! Keep the wind to your face on the way out! Enjoy the sunrises!

Sunrisers

Sunrisers

Table of Contents

<u>*Poems*</u>

I'll write them, if you'll read them

Let you interpret what you've read

The words, I put to paper, should bring thought into your head

I didn't miss a comma, there was no word left out

I purposely misspelled a word, to bring about, more thought

Mine rhyme, because I want them to, there is no master scheme

Some come to me while running, some come to me in dreams

I'll write them, if you'll read them

My explanation as to how they're formed

My thoughts just seem to come to me and they come to me in Poems

<u>*The Sunriser*</u>

Each morning, before the sunrises,
a parade of risers, make a journey, to the shores

Why are they heading to the ocean's edge
What is it there, that they have in store

Why the journey in the darkness
The sunriser has seen this before

The sunrise is never truly the same
It's made different by the ocean's roar

The sunriser can hear the ocean
In his thoughts mermaids and whales

As the sun takes to the sky
The sunriser bids the night farewell

Sun Painted Waves

The sun's rays touched its canvas

The waves, was the canvas, receiving the brush's strokes

*The sun painted waves glistened, with oranges and greens,
that could not be cloaked*

Each bristle of the sun's rays stroked the ocean

Each color reflected and returned toward the sky

The sun painted waves held, boundless, beauty

*The sunriser, lucky enough, to be able, to absorb the beauty, with
her eyes!*

Sunrisers

Sea Shells

Pushed and tumbling across the seas
The sands, beneath feet, were once as me

Broken from an elegant form
Grounded to grains by passing storms

Sometimes smooth and sometimes not
Placed on a shelf, a forget me not

There still is beauty possessed in each
As they wash ashore on every beach

Written by Kendall Thompson

Sunrise

One incredible moment

All things are blessed to share

Moving gracefully above the horizon

Bringing a glow and awesome glare

Waited on by millions

A pristine and lordly show

Preparing to provide the light of day

With its awe inspiring glow

In an Instant

It happened in an instant
The dusk became the dawn

The sun sprang up, just beyond the sea
The day star again was born

The clouds had shaded its brilliance
It could not shade it for long

The power of its awesome rays
Shone brilliantly and shone strong

It was only for an instant, when the night,
Suddenly became the day

Minutes pass, the instant happens again,
for someone else, for the instant cannot stay!

On Track

I had passed the halfway point,
In fact there were minutes left to go

The distance traveled along the route, hell,
I really don't know

I set out to reach the lighthouse,
It was now a distant view behind

I am headed back from whence I came, but
I can't seem to see the street signs

I was hot and I was sweating, the sand was soft, which made it
tough

I finally looked at my watch and I had run just enough

I had followed the tracks of tires
The lighthouse, the halfway mark

Good thing the tracks of tires remained; this is what led me back
to the start.

<u>Hammock in the Breeze</u>

Swinging slowly in a hammock, this soon, after a morning run

The breeze dried my clothes off, my toes, licked by the sun

The others, inside, are sleeping
Each vacation, owned by one's self

So mine is filled with running miles and
counting each beach access

Each beach access accounted for, I settle into an ease

I hear the sound of the ocean
I am laying in a hammock in a breeze

<u>The Final Run</u>

Bodies browned from sun kissed days

Recovering from a moonlit night

Travel, early, next morning, so it, was only right

Run while all were sleeping, even before the sun did rise

The beach was free of fishermen, sunrises, still focused their eyes

My final run is in the books, I left marks in the sand

This does not mean, the journey ends,
I will execute the master plan

I will run the dictated distance,
I will show up, when told, at the track

The final run, on this beach this year but the promise to self,
I'll be back

<u>*Vacation Town*</u>

Just like that, the town is empty
Each family makes their journey home

Cars are packed, kids buckled in
The house, now, all alone

The house, too, holds the memories
The memories each family made

The memory of the perfect wave,
reading books in instant shade

My hope, there was a journal,
To write in it, one not too young

I hope in twenty years, there is writing in the journal,
again, this time, by a not too young son's son

<u>On Deck</u>

Reclining on a deck of wood
A cold drink held firmly in hand

Overlooking the Ocean
Overlooking dunes of sand

Watching fishers fish
Dog walkers walking their dogs

Seeing a walker walking
A jogger has started his jog

On deck with friends and family
Enjoying a restful day

Waves crashing as the water washes ashore
Enjoying the ocean's spray!

Time on deck is priceless
No thoughts or thinking allowed

The drink in hand isn't water, this time
In the sky not a single cloud!

Sunrisers

The Ocean's Allure

The sounds of the crashing waves, they frighten me
I can hear the power that they possess

Their rapid return to the ocean is dizzying
I enter the waves, nonetheless

The lure of the water is amazing
The beckoning call of the sea

The crashing, of the waves, is calling out
I can hear them singing to me

In its sounds you can hear the power
In its return journey, back out to sea

The power it possesses is frightening
The waves also possess an alluring beauty!

<u>Almost Perfect</u>

The house backs up to the roadway
The bedroom door doesn't always lock

The noise, it doesn't bother me
Our children have learned to knock

The weather is dry and sunny
The cooler, stocked with cold drinks

If it rains, we will go into the water
If the cooler empties, we will perform restocking

Vacation is nearly perfect
Although it is almost done

There is a thing more I would like to do
I have made more times for more runs!

<u>Workout Vacation Run</u>

The first stride, taken in darkness
The last stride, while the sun was bright

Is it always the early bird that gets the worm
It was early and I was on a solo flight

The streets I ran, mostly vacant
There was another die hard or two

It took the warmup miles before another was seen
There wasn't more than that, before I was through

My task was to run hard when I was supposed to
Warm down when I was done

Follow the instructions of my running mate
Complete a workout vacation run!

Before it Rained

The waves were steadily crashing
The water, an emerald, like green

We are on the Emerald Isle,
so this makes perfectly good sense to me

The weather forecast spoke of thunderstorms
The storms would arrive shortly after dawn

The running part, of my vacation day,
would already, be completely done

The chance of precipitation, was a little above forty percent

The chance would increase, in the next hours
, but you see, I have already went

The weather forecast called for cloudy,
but this forecast was prior to dawn

I would get my workout in, before it rained, because I was
running, in the early morn

Well I thought I would get it in,
before it began to rain

It just would not, be in the cards, for me to finish, my workout,
before it rained!

Rare Footage

Our family in a photo
Rare footage, of them and me

On a beach vacation
Us, all together, is such a rarity

Conversation between the footage
A short video, to catch the sounds

They laughed and talked and talked and laughed
We wrote our names on the beach, sandy ground

Truly rare footage, of her and them, and me

Another family moment, I took pictures for great memories!

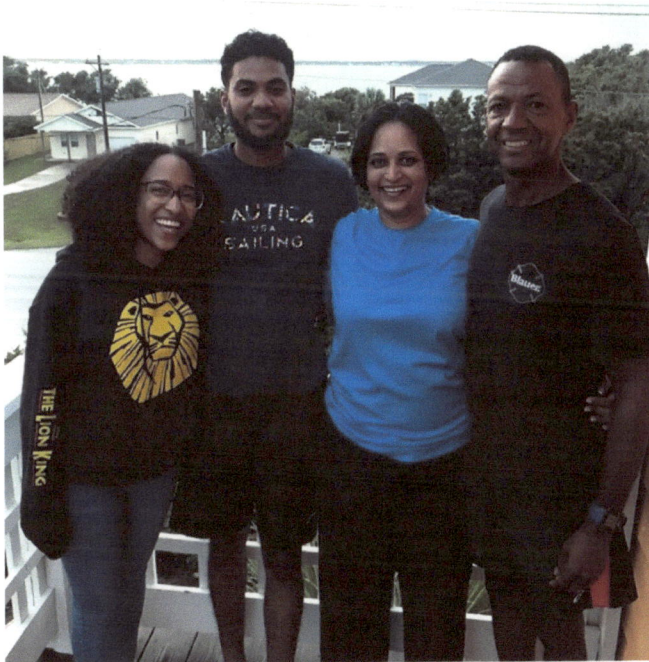

Emerald and Ocean Loop

The long sides were Emerald and Ocean
The short sides, second and twenty-fifth

The loop was four in total, so twice around is what I did

Eight miles run, in total
Five, run, before the sun woke up

Two ran in the pouring rain
The last one hot, so I sucked it up

The Emerald and Ocean loop
I felt it was aptly named

The emerald colored ocean with whistling winds

There is a chance I may have to run it again!

Cautiously Living

There would be no early morning exploring
There was no chance of me going out on a run

The sky was lit up, by lightning
The rain clouds, deluge, blocked the sun

I watched the waves, crash ashore, from the balcony
I listened, as the thunder, rocked the walls

I watched, in awe, of nature's forces, in hopes that the storm,
would not stall

The wind, rain, thunder, and lightning
Letting you know the earth is alive

Take cover and make sure you're cautious
Stay inside to ensure you'll survive!

It seems I have been listening for hours
The sounds of thunder, since a quarter pass four

My will to live, kept me cautious
Common sense made sure I didn't go out the door!

The Still Shot

The face may seem, to you, menacing
In a picture you can't see his heart

No smile, is this man angry
In real life, is he so hard

Maybe, just maybe, he is smiling
Smiling but the sun's in his eyes

Maybe you have only seen him smiling,
so this picture to you a surprise

The picture, shows one frame of some moments
The next moment, I bet there is a smile

The still shot, seen in a photograph, doesn't have the same affect,
of seeing him live!

<u>My Watch Watched</u>

Spending time on vacation
Surely I am not pressed for time

Watching my watch is something I do
I watch my watch, when I'm on mine

It is not that I am running late
It isn't that I have some where to be

I watch my watch to ensure I am keeping the pace
I watch it because the warm down seems too long to me!

So when I am on vacation and you see me keeping time

I am watching it to remain on pace
My watch watched to ensure I am running fine!

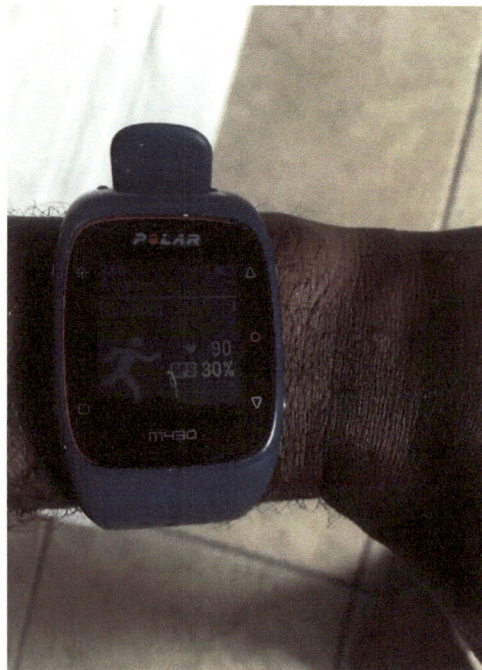

Taking Strides

The storm did pass on the island
There was a window for us to go outside

This was the moment we took action
This was the moment that we took our strides

It has been years since we ran together
Well we have been running around together, before the age of five

My cousin and I, together again
Hanging at the beach and running strides

Today just another chapter
Our lives have intersected our entire lives

Today we got to run together again
We went out after the storm and took our strides!

The Return Flight

The initial takeoff was a bit bumpy
Hell, the return flight was no picnic

The out and back was turbulent
The workout an experience

Hard is an understatement
I would not hit, one benchmark

I do have one thing to be proud of
I finished the entire workout

The initial takeoff, a bit bumpy
The return flight was just as hard

The cut down times did occur
Even though the times were quite a bit off!

Sunrisers

Measured in Smiles

How is happiness measured
Is it measured in ounces and pounds

I feel it is measured in smiles,
in laughter and joyous sounds

The success of a family outing
Smiles that stretch from ear to ear

Laughing and joking with one another
Storytelling for all to share

How is your happiness measured
We measure our happiness in smiles

See our smiles stretched from ear to ear
We made certain ours would last for a while!

Friends

There is thunder in the distance
The sun is bright overhead

A chance to visit a longtime friend
A story or two, with beers in our hand

We hugged and smiled, for we had made it
In our lives we had helped others who were in need

Now a moment to relax ourselves,
a moment to share our memories

We spoke of old captains and chiefs
Battalion and Department Heads

We spoke of drivers and sergeants
We spoke of those living and those now dead

We hugged again and laughed
We swore we would see each other again

Most of all we enjoyed our time
We spent our time with our longtime friend!

Peaceful Transition

It happens every morning
It happens without a fight

There is peaceful transition, as the day, takes over for the night

There is no quarrel, the night doesn't put up a fight

The nighttime understands that it's time is up
and it must give way to daylight

So there is a peaceful transition
The night makes way for the day

The nighttime knows that it's time has come
There is no need for it to try and remain!

So we enjoy a peaceful transition
The daytime takes over for the night

The nighttime knows it's time has come and graciously
transitions to daylight!

Racing the Tide

The beachfront was rapidly disappearing
The waves ate, vociferously, yards of sand

I would run an eight mile, out and back
At least that was my original plan

On the route I saw a harem of wild horses
So I chased, until I got out in front

Those who know me best, know this next quote
"I wasn't eating them, so, I was running from"

This added miles to my run
I would end up getting my clothes and shoes wet

Well, on this day, I would end up beating the tide
I wasn't wet from water but I was drenched in sweat!

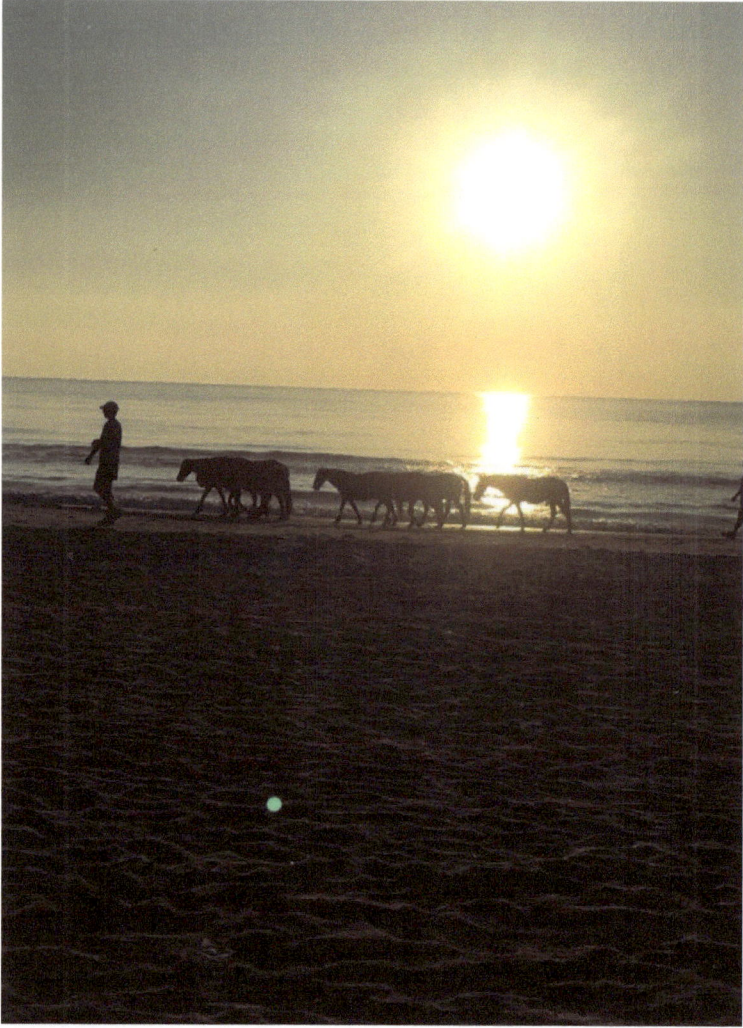

The Ocean's Edge

I sat on the edge of the ocean
In my palms I held the sands of time

I sat where both shells and stones alike, come to eternally lie

I listened as the waves crashed ashore
I watched, as the sun breached the clouds

I wondered if there was a heaven
I wondered this question aloud

I thought about evolution
I remembered, it was said, he created both the heavens and the
earth

I heard the whispers of the crashing waves
I watched the flight of the sea birds

I watched as other humans made ready
As each marked an area in the sand

I watched as the sun took over
I questioned was this ocean the birth place of man?

<u>*Remnants of Sea Turtles*</u>

In my hands I held the sands time
Each handful, washed away by a wave

What was in each handful
What was being washed away

Was there remnants of sea turtles
In my hands, was there bits of pearls and sharks' teeth

Was there mollusks, crustaceans, and other natantia

What was in the sand that covered my feet

In my hands I held the sands of time
Eons, held in the palms, of my hands

The remnants of shells that washed ashore

Now being washed away with each grain of sand!

<u>Foggy</u>

I was late, but I didn't miss it
I would have to wait for the fog to clear

I took this as a gentle reminder, that we've had a tumultuous year

The fog may be clouding our vision but the sun
seems to always rise

I watched as it burned the fog away, this happened before my eyes

The waves still rolled up the beaches
The birds still took to flight

Although I couldn't see the sun's rise
I saw that it pushed out the night

Let's not wait for the fog to clear
The sun has risen and it won't be long

It only took minutes for the sun to rise
It was seconds before the fog was long gone!

Sunrisers

<u>Peacefully Loud</u>

The waves were peacefully loud, as they crashed upon the shore

The clouds, were formed, in the distance,
waiting to show their force

The lightning, that shone eight hours ago, now gone

I am waiting for the sun to spring up from behind the clouds

The waves are crashing onto the shore, and they sure are
peacefully loud

The hawkeyed osprey have taken to flight to find, a fish,
its next meal

I watch, in utter amazement, as the sun risers,
await the visual thrill

Waiting for the sun to rise above the distant clouds

Listening to the waves crash ashore
They sure are peacefully loud!

<u>*Drift Wood*</u>

Where have I once traveled
What destinations, for me, to come

I have landed on a crowded beach
Where have I landed from

Is this my final journey
Will the next wave wisp me away

Will I find a location, that I will get to stay

Will the tide's rise come reach me
Will this happen soon

I look forward to drifting away
I look forward to my next dune!

<u>Nature Made</u>

The waves was the music that I ran to
The wind was the partner with which I danced

The sunrise was our chaperone
The soft sand ensured that I was being romanced

The dance floor was on the edge of the ocean
It was covered with remnants of shells

The music of the waves, though peaceful, was just loud enough
that I'd have to yell

The drift wood would act as the wall flower, unless a wave would
come to take its hand

All things described and considered
I was dancing to the sound of nature's live band

So I ran and I danced with the wind
I listened to loud music by the waves

I was chaperoned by each and every sunrise
Each melody was nature made!

Sunrisers

Tearless Grief

As I sit and watch the sunrise, my morning full of glee

*I sit back and I wonder, are there really angels,
watching over me?*

I think about dead loved ones often and our countless memories

I sit and try to cry but can't,

I guess it's not destined for me to grieve

Pondering about life and death, will I really be just a corpse?

*Is there a great beyond, reincarnation, or do you just get taken
away with no remorse?*

*At the young age of twenty-two, I'm nowhere close to where I
want to be*

*Will I be successful, fulfill my dreams, before those guardian
angels are me?*

Written by Kendall Thompson Jr

The Ferrying of Sand

Each beach trip we ferry sand
This year no ferry will be made

It isn't that it was made illegal
It isn't that we are afraid

The ferrying of sand won't happen, but the memory of why we
ferried remains

In each grain of sand ferried, a memory was ingrained

We ferried sand to my sister, we ferried sand along with shells

This year there will be no ferrying
No moment to tell her our tales

We won't ferry for she didn't request it
Wait this doesn't make a bit of sense

Let me rush back to the beach and grab some shells
The shells will still be ferried, ferrying the sand will have to be
heaven sent!

<u>*Dancing Clouds*</u>

The clouds were dancing above the waves
The clouds danced beneath the rising sun

The waves were painted by the sunrise
The winds pushed the clouds from where they'd come

Some clouds would dance together
Some clouds danced in groups of five

An orchestrated, recital, the dancing clouds made certain that we
were alive

The waves being painted by the sunrise
The wind pushed the clouds from where they came

The clouds danced above the waves and below the clouds the
waves did the same!

Photo by Victoria Thompson

<u>The Fox Trot</u>

The fox trot, occurred each morning
It must have lived within the dunes

The fox would trot along the ocean's edge
The beach must have been its living room

The fox would trot amongst the people
It would chase and maybe, catch a wayward bird

I didn't see a bird being caught
This was learned, by overheard words

The fox stood still for a picture
Me, on the on the other hand, I continued on

The fox trot equates to a dance
On this day, the fox trot, occurred with the rise of the sun

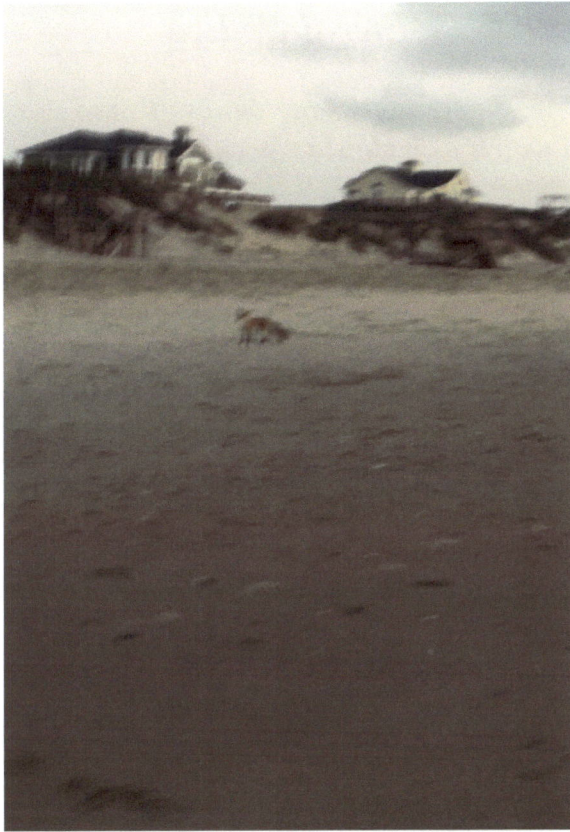

<u>Eternity's Eye</u>

I peer across the dunes of sand
I watch as it slowly rises above the waves

I think about our next tomorrow
I will only remember some of our yesterdays

This is the beauty in each sunrise
This is the beauty in each wave

Each will come in and each will go
By another, it will be replaced

I peer across the dunes of sand, into the eye of eternity

As I peer across the dunes of sand
Eternity's eye peers back at me

Heaven's Meadow

The dunes of sand are the fences to heaven's meadows

The rolling waves, the pastures', fields of green

The sun warms the sand and the shallow waters

The force of water, creates temporary streams

The meadow was well lit by a heavenly light

The light was not the sun, just yet, it was the moon

I am walking to the edge of the ocean
The rise of the sun, will happen, very soon!

Sunrisers

<u>*Acknowledgement*</u>

*Thank you to my wife and children, who tolerate the early bird
who wants to get the worm! Thank you for sleeping through my
noise. Thanks to PJ Devlin for getting me to my writer's paradise.
Thank you to Lynn Nelson, Roberta Elliot Speight, and Black
Roots Alexandria for your constant support. Thank you to the
willing and unwilling faces that appear in this book. Thank you to
Phil Devereaux and to my cousin, Lorna Lewis Eaton, for being
in this book of verse. Thank you Phil for the photo.
Thank you, one and all, for believing in me. Thanks for reading
my stuff.*

ABOUT THE AUTHOR

Kendall Thompson dedicated his life to protecting his community as a Firefighter. He's a member of a proud African American family with deep roots in Alexandria, Virginia and a history of community service. Kendall is a long-distance runner and family man. His poems spring from his soul and are about his thoughts at a particular moment. The author loves when others have thoughts from reading his poems. He likes to say," thanks for reading my stuff!"

Peacefully Loud is the author's fifth book of verse. He has also written WHY WE WALK IN THE STREET, Angry Black Man, Hearing Whispers, and REVERED.